Victor Contoski

NAMES

OTHER BOOKS BY VICTOR CONTOSKI

POETRY

BROKEN TREATIES (New Rivers Press, 1973)

TRANSLATIONS

Jerzy Harasymowicz, *PLANTING BEECHES*
(New Rivers Press, 1975)
Tadeusz Rosewicz, *UNEASE*
(New Rivers Press, forthcoming, fall 1979)

Victor Contoski

NAMES

New Rivers Press 1979

Copyright © 1979 by Victor Contoski
Library of Congress Catalog Card Number: 79-64150
ISBN 0-89823-007-1
All Rights Reserved
Typesetting: John Minczeski
Book Design: C. W. Truesdale

Special thanks to the editors of these magazines in which some of these poems appeared for the first time: *Epoch*, *Everybody's Ex-Lover*, *Harrison Street Review*, *Isthmus*, *Kayak*, *The Minnesota Review*, *New Letters*, *Poetry Now*, *Quixote*, *Specialia*, *Tampa Poetry Review*, *Tractor*, *Shenandoah*, and *Wild Dog*. Some of these poems were included in *31 New American Poets* (Hill & Wang, 1969). Special thanks also to the Toledo Museum of Art, Toledo, Ohio for permission to reproduce photographs of African Masks in that collection.

NAMES has been published with the aid of generous grants from the National Endowment for the Arts and the New York State Council on the Arts.

New Rivers Press Books are distributed by
        SBD: Small Press Distribution
        Jeanetta Jones Miller
        1636 Ocean View Avenue
        Kensington, California
        94707

NAMES has been manufactured in the United States of America for New Rivers Press (C. W. Truesdale, Editor/Publisher), 1602 Selby Avenue, St. Paul, Minnesota 55104 in a first edition of 750 copies of which 15 have been signed and numbered by the author.

NAMES

I

11. Names
12. Word
13. Desk
14. The Months
15. Stock Market Poem
16. Hatred
17. Shoes
19. Thought
20. Work
21. Dirty Thoughts
22. Gray Building
23. Hangover
24. Prayer
25. Grief
26. Pain

II

29. The King Of The Poison Mushrooms
31. Autumn
32. Amanitas
33. The Fingertips Of The Dead
34. Dead Man's Cup
35. Dutch Elm Disease
36. Walk In The Woods
37. The Constellations Of Autumn
38. Protest
39. November
40. The Suicides Of The Rich

41. Elegy
42. The Message
43. Loss
44. Poem For One Who Died In The Night
45. December Afternoon
46. Snowstorm

III

49. Letter
50. Pain In My Hand
51. The Enemy
52. The Sack
60. The Tall Buildings Of Manhattan
62. Energy
63. Witnesses
64. Teddy Bear
65. Game 23
66. The Arab-Israeli Six-Day War
70. Exile
71. Trashing

IV

75. Exercises For The Tongue
76. Elegy For A Rooster
77. Egg Poem
78. Paper Poem
79. Sunrise
80. Perspective
81. Those I Love
82. Cause And Effect
83. The First Animal
84. Lust
85. Birthday Poem
86. Clock

87. Opera Season
88. Sorrow
90. Biting My Fingernails
91. Honor
92. Morning Poem
93. Return
94. Summer Night

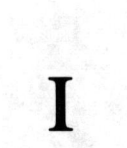

I

NAMES

If I knew the names
I would ask them:
    Why do you stand here
    waiting
    at the edge of winter
    with such inhuman patience,
    your arms outstretched
    to the darkness?

If I knew the names
I would tell them:
    What has fallen
    has fallen.

WORD

Since before the fall of empires
I have held it in my mouth like a kiss

and there it has grown
feeding on my tongue

growing fat on the hollows of my cheeks
to no purpose but its appetite.

Neither angel, star, nor trumpet
shall summon it to existence

but its cue shall be the entry
of the king with the bleeding eyes

and the slow offstage tread
of the stone gods approaching.

And as my lips part for screaming
it will gather its strength

tear down the teeth and tumble
blackly toward the sun like a bird.

And the shadow of its wings
shall fall like death on the people

those good people
kneeling in tears
crying:
> *yes*
> *yes.*

DESK

Dark and beautiful it lies
under a white paper moon
remembering its forests.

All night it murmurs
like a sleepy girl to her lover
of what it knew and loved
in the old country.

THE MONTHS

Their feet are drums.

We line the sidewalks,
our hands full of flags.

Faithful servants,
they intone
over the sound of their boots,
take this and this and this.

And then they are gone
and their gifts are gone

and we are old.

STOCK MARKET POEM

Numbers speak
in the language of numbers.

They stand waiting
like beautiful girls.

Take us, they say. *We're yours.*
We're innocent, all of us.
It will be the first time.

And their hands are out for money.

We look into their eyes
and see our daughters
who left home years ago
following a man
into a mountain.

HATRED

It hurts
it hurts

deep down
where I never knew I had nerves
it burrows in and hangs on
gnawing out for itself
a festering kingdom
like a bad tooth

like two bad teeth
that I grind in hatred.

SHOES

1

Entering my shoes is like
entering the woman I love.

Every morning I tie them to my feet
like wrapping presents to myself.

2

If you love someone
don't give your heart.
Give your shoe.
Like Cinderella.

3

When Daedalus made himself wings
he was unfaithful to his shoes.

They never forgot.
They killed his son.

4

When Jesus walked on the water
He went barefoot.

In the Garden of Olives

when Judas kissed Him
he also stepped on His toe.

5

An evil magician ran a string
through the eyeballs of beautiful girls
to make himself a necklace.

The eyes of my shoes are beautiful and blind.

6

My feet have long since lost the road
but my shoes know the way.

When I kneel down they point into the ground.
I will die with them on.

THOUGHT

1

It begins
by sneaking into my room,

avoiding my traps with hunks
of silence over their hooks.

When my back is turned
it grabs me by the ears,

throws me to the ground,
tears off my clothes,

covers me with hot, wet kisses
and expects me to make love.

2

Then I take it in my arms
as if I really cared,

all the time looking for leverage
to apply the cross-body hammer hold
I learned from the Java Indians.

3

As our lips meet its guard goes down.
Suddenly my hands twist.

Give? Give? I cry
but the only sound
is the crack of bones.

I lower it gently to the ground
sobbing *Give?* There is no answer.

I put its body with the others.

WORK

I carry it with me
in my pockets
useless as pennies.

When I salute the dead,
applaud my contemporaries,
or hold out my palms
to those I love
suddenly I find
my hands are full of it.

Wherever I live it is there
in the next room waiting
patient as a friend
with bad news.

DIRTY THOUGHTS

Priests told me they were my enemies
so when I was young I rebuffed them,
excluded them from my parties
and cut them cold in the street.

If they wept,
they wept in private.

Their quiet patience
outlasted my friends.
Their simplicity
put my lovers to shame.

Through the years
I have grown
accustomed to them.

They are here now.

If you are very quiet
you can hear them
in the next room
singing.

GRAY BUILDING

The spell of the windows is broken.
The old wooden boards are dreaming of matches.

The white paint has left for heaven
with the souls of the faithfully departed.

Hat in hand I mount the pitted cement steps
looking for my childhood.

The sign on the door says:
This building has been condemned.

HANGOVER

It
is morning.

I hang my feet over the edge
and they disappear.

Memory comes back
masked,
the knife still in his hand,
demanding his money.

My house is overrun by cactus.

PRAYER

They told me to listen
in the stillness
and I listened.

Ghosts of buffalo
held their breath,
and the flow of blood ceased.

Rust formed.
Mildew grew,
and her hair fell softly
strand by strand.

And I heard the voice of the silence
as was foretold to me

the great voice of the silence
saying nothing.

GRIEF

When I was introduced to Grief
I was prepared for anything
but the joy-buzzer in his hand.

They laughed.

He slapped my back and slid
the chair out from under me,
and there I was on my bottom
right in the middle of the room.

What does it mean? I asked.

Nothing, he whispered.
Then the tears came.
Now you know. Nothing.

PAIN

Pain lives in a house
by the side of the road.

Only the regulars
know her number.

Her girls solicit so quietly
hardly anyone suspects them.

Yet one day when you are lost
you will knock on a door

hoping for directions
and there will be Pain.

And her beautiful, evil daughters
who have long desired your body

will take you in their arms.

II

POISON MUSHROOMS

THE KING OF THE POISON MUSHROOMS

1

In the first faint light of dawn
the King of Poison Mushrooms
surveys his mist and moss,
while up through dead leaves and grass
his henchmen poke their grey thumbs.

People silent as ghosts
slide through the forest
to pay him tribute.

2

Here the unwary ignore him
but underground he is Pluto's equal.

3

A young girl reaches down,
her hand on his skin like rain.
He closes his eyes and dreams
she is Lucretia Borgia.

4

His beautiful deadly daughter
is ripe for marriage.

Throughout the day
suitors arrive
to guess her riddle.

No one has ever succeeded.

As the sun sets
she kisses them.

5

And at night
the King of Poison Mushrooms
stands in our dreams
tall as a telephone pole
claiming those we love
as his subjects.

They close their eyes
and put out their tongues
to receive him.

AUTUMN

I

On the overgrown road
where nobody comes
autumn is an old abandoned house.

The blank walls sag,
lean trembling
as if undecided which way to fall.

They have no color but grey,
the bone color.

Their dampness
is not of this century.

But the house shall not fall.
Ever.

II

Ages ago the wind broke the panes
and planted the glass
that has not yet come up
but is growing surely,
germinating in the mud.

That glass will one day bloom,
poke out through the clay
like blades,
flourish in the sun

and stand like bushes
of cheap jewelry
waiting to ambush a traveler
who has not come for centuries
and probably will never come.

The spangled bushes!
If anyone were alive
he would think they burn.

But they are cold.

Birds shall eat of them
and die.

AMANITAS

Last night
through mist and fog and darkness
the hand of God reached down
and touched the grass.

All we have now
are His fingerprints:
little white angels of death.

THE FINGERTIPS OF THE DEAD

Plant the fingertips of the dead
in a cool, dark place. Pray over them.
They will come up through the ground
like mushrooms. Poison, of course,
but beautiful. Beautiful.

They touch our faces like lovers,
leaving cool spots, white as frostbite,
that will never be warm.

DEAD MAN'S CUP

for Bob Schrag

The woman who loved him
puts his cup in my hands.

It is cold.

I fill it with black tea.
The leaves tell me nothing.

As I lift the dead man's cup
light vanishes.

On my lips
the tea is warm.

DUTCH ELM DISEASE

1

Not even the elms
are above suspicion.

They sway in the wind
as if dancing,

but some may well be dead.
Come spring we will know.

2

Others have taken
the worm to their hearts.

Only the moles at their roots
hear them gasping for breath

and the moles are silent.

WALK IN THE WOODS

For the love of wood
I kneel down
and offer it my hands.

If I am very still
and wait a long time
bark will grow over them.

THE CONSTELLATIONS OF AUTUMN

The constellations of autumn
rise silently over my house
breathing the music of names
given them long ago
by dead astronomers:
>*Algol*
>*Capella*
>*Elnath.*

My wife breathes
in her sleep.

From August grass
rises the whispered clicking
of crickets.

Each is saying its own name
over and over and over.

Soft and steady
the words pulse
out into the darkness
like light
from the stars.

PROTEST

The leaves
have been protesting for some time,
stammering *justice*!
      in their foreign accents,
writing the same ungrammatical letters
      year after year,
parading their children,
waving their banners with the one word,
      now!

Throwing their hands to heaven
      like Guernica

and yet they fall.

NOVEMBER

1

There are no colors
under the November moon.

All is black and white
like an allegory.

2

The tree before you is paper thin.
Blow and it will bend.

Touch it at the edge
and you will cut your finger.

But you cannot touch the moon.
The moon is made of dry ice.

3

It is November
and you have done nothing.

The spit in your throat is freezing.
You are a fixed constellation.

Down at your feet the moon
throws your shadow like a quarter.

THE SUICIDES OF THE RICH

In autumn
the rich all over the world
are burdened by their bodies.

They fold their Wall Street Journals
and look dreamily toward the horizon.

And pistols find their hands.
Injections caress their braceleted arms.
Waves wash their tailored suits.

Wherever you go in autumn
you hear the soft *plop plop*
of the bodies of the rich
falling falling falling.

ELEGY

All afternoon snow falls
on the death of a good man.

I put my cheek to earth
as to a pillow.

Deep, deep underground
the dead are singing.

Love is their song.
I can barely hear it.

THE MESSAGE

The books are bent,
their pages loose.

Hands come apart.
Fingers flutter down.
Hair falls.

Tongues wrap themselves
around seeds.

A bob white
in the far field.

The unseen
sings
to the unreal.

LOSS

It is dark,
getting darker.
Now it is night.

Those with legs pack them up
and send them over the roads;
those with eyes
take them in their hands.

All those who love
lie down on the road
believing

and the heavy black wheel of the sky
rolls over them.

POEM FOR ONE WHO DIED IN THE NIGHT

Dreaming of the death
of your father
you step slowly
into running water.

And your legs are gone.
Clothes stick to your body
as if they mattered.

Water embraces your thighs
like a bandage.

Your hands are heavy.
Lay them in water.

Your tongue
is a smooth stone.

white water
over your face
like a sheet.

You are
still breathing.

DECEMBER AFTERNOON

Dirty snow like scabs
on the brown fields.

December is cold as steel.
You cannot move your lips.

Light droops in the house
like a pet slowly dying.

SNOWSTORM

Sleep is good.

Cold and soft as love
snow falls on my eyelashes.

I close my eyes
and look through the lids.

There will be many deaths
before the snow melts to water

and starts its slow journey
down my cheeks like tears.

Deep underground the seed
is doing its time.

Come March I shall have been dead
one hundred years.

III

STORIES OF ANCIENT CIVILIZATIONS

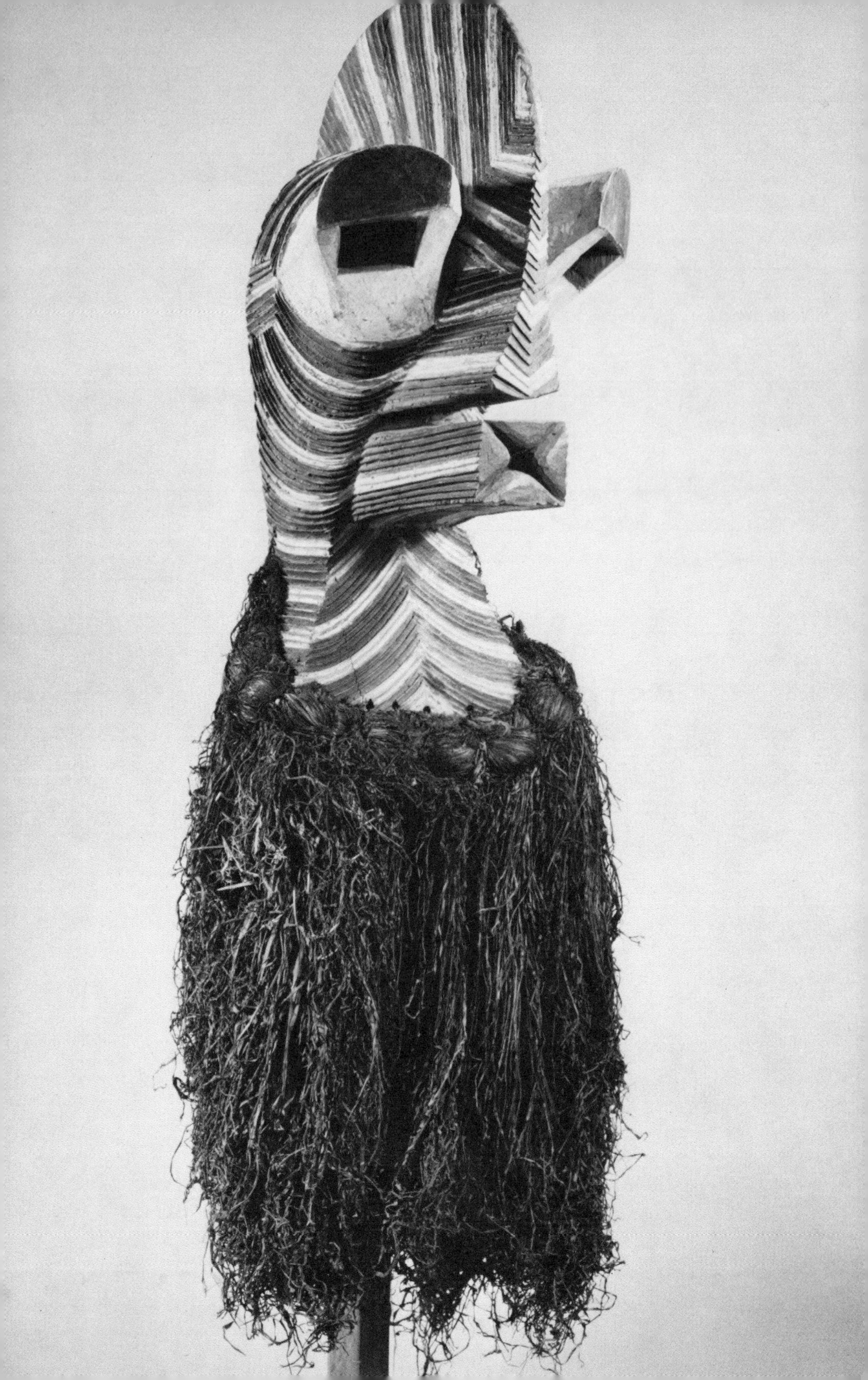

LETTER

You left behind you
a black book in the corner
The Story of Ancient Civilizations

tales of butcher-heroes
maimed captives
women weeping
and God
lapping the blood
of His children.

Hope you like your job
in the new country.

Just thought I'd tell you
it's still here
gathering dust
in the ruins

that black book.

PAIN IN MY HAND

1

My hand aches.

I turn it over
like a dead fish
searching for the hook.

No sign of blood.
No discoloration.

And yet the pain.
The pain.

2

A nail went through it centuries ago.

Rusted and flaking, invisible
it still keeps its trust
like a sentry making his rounds
in an outpost of the empire
not knowing the capitol has fallen.

THE ENEMY

The generals died in disgrace.
The policemen were shot.

It couldn't have been them.

The informers are dead of overdoses
and Congress committed suicide as a body
when exposed by the people.

Now there are only two of us left.

So it was you, friend, all along.

THE SACK

1
Happy Birthday

The happiness we deserve!

The sack is heavy, hard to lift.
We heave it up on the table,
open it, and there
we find Gilda dying.

She coughs blood
all over the sack.

2
Prehistory

The youngest son takes a sack with him
into the hill, slides it under his shirt,
stuffs it with food, then slits it open.
A giant kills himself for a sack.

The youngest son comes out a hero
holding the sack like a princess.

3
Troy

Towers falling in flames around him,
Aeneas looks frantically for his old father,
puts him in a sack and trudges through carnage,

the weight on his back pushing him earthward,
down, down, like the stones of the palace.

Stumbling into the woods
he sighs and puts the sack down.

Out comes a skeleton,
fleshless arms, beak-like head.
Thin bones fall on the sack
like dice.

4
Rome

Attila marches down over the Alps
raping and robbing and burning.

Pope Leo comes to see him.
Attila shows him a sack.

"How much will it hold?"
"Italy and then some."

5
The Middle Ages

The statues of the ancients
go into the sack.
Centuries later some emerge
noses off eyes knocked out
arms broken legs broken necks broken.

The wisdom of the ancients
goes into the sack
and comes out in fragments.

The ancients themselves
go into the sack
and never come out.

6
Inquisition

Soldiers and priests rush in.
"Nobody move. You're all under arrest."
They stuff everything into a sack,
throw it on the fire.

"But there's a woman . . ."

"No mistake.
Burn, witch! Burn!"

7
Sanctification

Centuries later
the flames die down.

An old man sifts the ashes
and finds a sack untouched by fire.

He picks it up
and his rheumatism is gone.

A crippled child touches it
and walks without crutches.

A leper touches it
and walks away whole.

8
Prayer for the Feast of the Sack

"Let whatever I was go into the sack.
Let it lie there with perished knowledge.
Let it lie with the body of Gilda.

When my time comes to enter
let there be darkness
and let the sack close over me
according to its will.

And may I enter
as though it were a door."

9
Lucretia Borgia

As she prays
a small sack of poison powder
hangs by a silver chain
from the neck of Lucretia Borgia

nestling between her breasts
like a jewel.

When lovers touch her body
she feels it move
against her skin
like a caress.

10
Benedict Arnold

Dying in England
Benedict Arnold
gestures for the sack
on the top shelf.

Inside
his old uniform
from the Continental Army.

With great pain
he reaches out
takes it
panting and wheezing
and rises from the bed.

Holding the uniform
in his trembling hands
as if it were infected
he totters to the fireplace
and throws it on the fire.

Arms outstretched he stumbles
back toward the bed.

He staggers
and falls.

Like a young man
touching a girl
for the first time
his wrinkled hand
caresses the sack.

and he dies.

11
Adolph Hitler

People are standing in line
to be shot,
standing in line
to be gassed:

young girls with braces on their teeth
mothers in plain dresses
old women with shawls on their heads
solemn boys with glasses
staring straight ahead
young men with stubble on their faces
old men with canes shaking their heads.

An SS trooper collects their clothing
for the good people of the Third Reich.

A dentist waits impatiently
to check the bodies
for gold teeth.

And young German recruits
stand by with scissors.

Hitler will use the bodies for soap.

Their hair will make a sack
big enough to hold
all the Jews in the world.

12
Richard Nixon

Richard Nixon puts his official memos
deep down into the sack.
He puts in his secret tapes
and incriminating papers.

He puts H. R. (Bob) Haldeman
into the sack.

He puts in Pat and Tricia
and Julie Nixon Eisenhower.

With tears in his eyes
he bids goodbye
to all that he loves.

In comes John Ehrlichman.
Nixon shakes his hand.

"For the good of the country."
"Of course."

The chief of protocol
discreetly ties the mouth of the sack.

Cameras whir.
Trumpets blare.
The U. S. Marine Band strikes up
"The Stars and Stripes Forever."

War widows strew flowers.

Ehrlichman tries to lift the sack.
But the official memos
the secret tapes

the incriminating papers
H. R. (Bob) Haldeman
Pat and Tricia
and Julie Nixon Eisenhower
are too heavy for him.

So down the flower-strewn carpet
to the Potomac River
beads of sweat on his forehead
John Ehrlichman rolls the sack
bit by bit
like Sisyphus.

13
Apotheosis

And look
up in the night sky
near the Northern Cross

a dark hole in the Milky Way
the Coal-sack Nebula.

14
Love Poem

Naked under the Coal-sack Nebula
I come to you in the darkness.

THE TALL BUILDINGS OF MANHATTAN

1

Dawn comes up over the East River,
over the skyscrapers of Manhattan.

Far out into America, into the Alleghenies,
the central woodlands, and the prairies
stretch the long shadows of tall buildings
like the fingers of their owners.

2

High up in great apartments
live men so rich
nobody knows their names.

They see only each other.

Their food goes up in baskets.
Their excrement comes down.

3

Their fragile women
gather on balconies
combing long, soft hair.

Far below they see
the sons of the poor
like little toy figures.

They let their hair down.

It reaches only
to the 27th floor.

Like dumb beasts
the sons of the poor
cry and turn away.

4

They turn inland to make their fortunes,
dreaming of the hair of New York women.

And the long, long shadows
of the tall buildings of Manhattan
fall on their backs like whips.

INSCRIPTION ON AN ABANDONED BASE

For years Americans held me against men
thinking men were their enemies.
Now I have fallen to moss.

ENERGY

All day it traveled over the prairies on foot
looking furtively for some sign of its relatives,
for friendly Indians or tracks of a caravan.

It hid where it could
in gullies, in thickets
when there were thickets.

When there were none
it lay flat.

And night descended
with new words
like Cold and Change.

But finally it came home
with its tongue cut out.
Home with its eyes gone
its hands lopped off
to find father dead
mother dead
brother murdered
sister missing
and only the lovers still there
under the charred bed
waiting. . .

WITNESSES

In sunlight
you cannot see them,
but they are there
like stars.

They go with the scenery:
    hair like woodwork,
    backs like buildings,
    feet blend with the grass.

In gutters
you cannot distinguish them
from snow.

They sleep at night in fields
till the bulldozers come.

In late summer
they migrate to the country
to die.

At night
when the machines are quiet
you can hear them in the grass
like crickets
whispering:
    justice,
    justice.

TEDDY BEAR

Fate sits on the sofa
in a lump:

button eyes
thread nose
guts of cloth
that will never love you.

GAME 23

A naked woman and a dead dwarf
on the carpet in an empty room.

She lies on her back
fresh from bathing.
Her breasts move
as she breathes.

Opposite, a dead dwarf
in blood-smeared yellow rags
face-down on a broken nose,
his hump over him like a stone.

Then: trumpets and drums.

The door of the room opens
and the lover enters
blindfolded, mouth puckered,
hands outstretched and groping. . .

THE ARAB-ISRAELI SIX-DAY WAR

1. *Preparation*

The armies have been training for years.
They are poised in the wings
like dancers listening for cues.

A roll of drums.
A clash of cymbals.

They lean forward
like a hungry man
leans over a steak.

2. *Outbreak of Hostilities*

Morning.
It is silent on the desert.
Nobody breathes.
War has not started.

Through the early hours
terrorists have killed quietly.
The bodies are still upright
afraid to fall for the noise.

Then
far away
like popcorn
the eggs of airplanes
start hatching.

3. *Artillery Battle*

Huge dynamite balloons
float carefully through villages
destroying good children
and innocent women.

Naughty children dance through the rubble.
Unfaithful wives lie safely abed
with their cowardly lovers.

In the hills
soldiers play cards.
The artillery battle goes on
automatically.

4. *Tank Battle*

Tanks advance on each side
like rows of checkers.
They would like nothing better
than to pair off,
wander out in the desert,
and make love.

They rumble onward
in fire and smoke
cursing the inhuman men
who drive them.

They run down.
Nobody winds them up.

Now they are burning.

They turn on their sides
like tired children
and die.

5. *Battle at the Pass*

No one can get through.
Traffic jam.

Bombs.

The generals get out and run.
The good metal stays at its post.

6. *Retreat*

The fleeing soldiers have taken off their shoes.
They have taken off their feet.
Their hands lie down and die.
Eyes, ears, and hair
run off in all directions.

7. *Negotiations*
(to be arranged)

brave defenders of the fatherland
fruits of aggression
the cause of peace
dawn of a new era
Arab people of Palestine
International Zionism
the right of a free people

widows
orphans
dead heroes

we will never compromise
we will never agree

coda.
da capo al fine.

8. *Epilogue*

Night falls
on the Sinai
like a soldier.

Far far away
in the darkness
something
still smoulders.

The wind crawls
over the desert
and stares.

EXILE

He went
the symbol of sorrow
into that huge country
knowing neither language
nor custom

to remain
always
the stranger among strangers

to stand in his age
straight as a board
with lancers
of the non-existent army.

TRASHING

Four a.m.
Open the curtains.

Light!
Stars risen like Christs
white and singing.

Scorpio with the moon in its tail,
the moon, the moon,
the moon in its tail.

Antares
the moon.
Dschubba
the moon.
Shaula
the moon.

The sopranos of the Milky Way
sing: *White! White!*

They have held their notes
through the darkness of centuries.

White! White!

And windows are breaking
all over America.

IV

EXERCISES FOR THE TONGUE

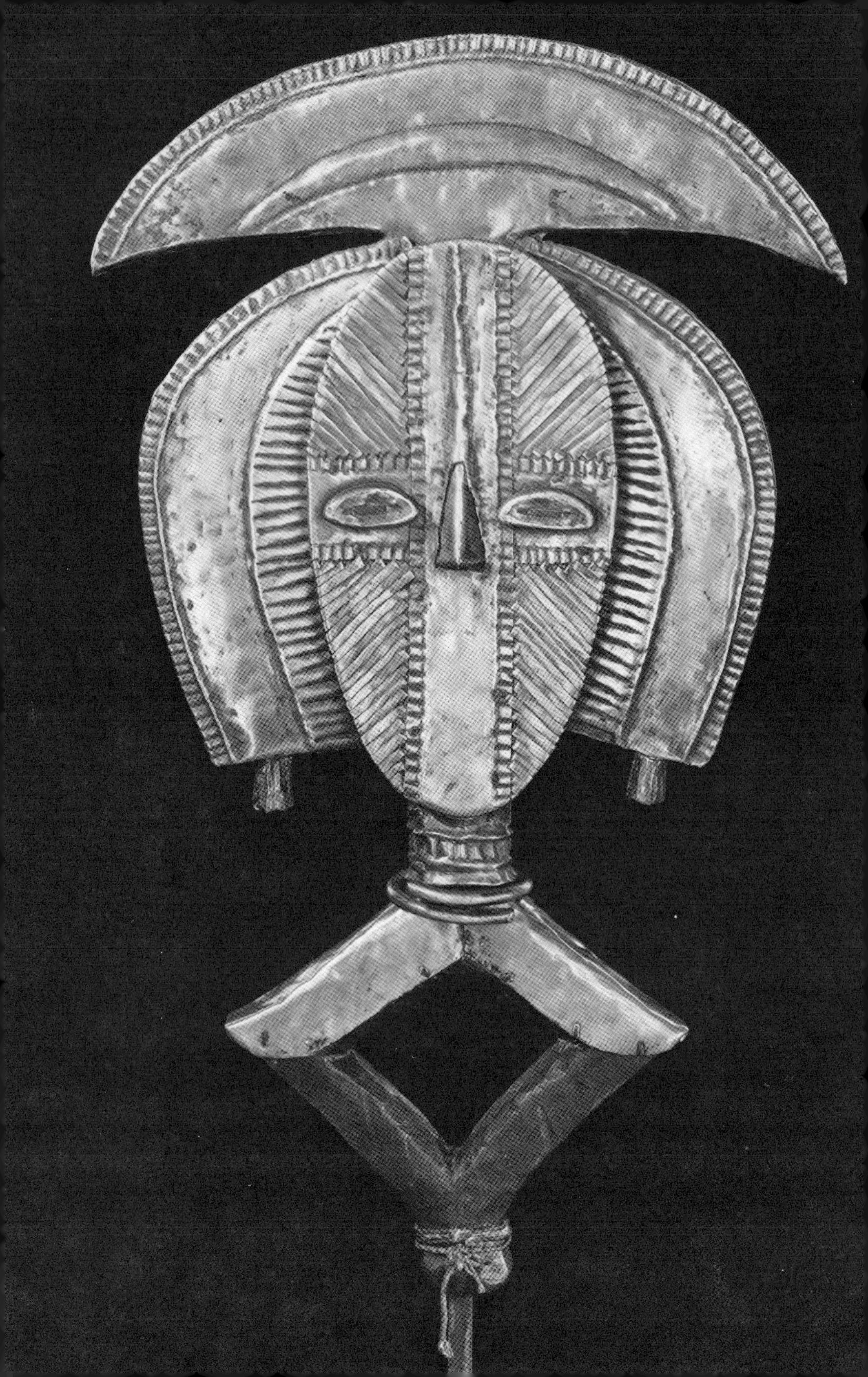

EXERCISES FOR THE TONGUE

1

Recite the Declaration of Independence.
Practice shoving meat between your teeth.
Say *shibboleth*.

2

Like a blind man
trying to remember
someone's features
touch thoroughly
the one you love.

3

Take a magnifying glass and a mirror.
Examine the calm country of your tongue.

Note the statesman by its fountains.
Note the poets and philosophers in its caves.
In its meadows note the lovers happy ever after.

4

On the broad expanse of its plains
two generals emerge from their tents
preparing to review the Continental Army.

"Good morning," says General George Washington.
"Good morning," says General Benedict Arnold.

ELEGY FOR A ROSTER

Year after year
the faces slide from the names.

Who wrote *come* and went
Who said goodbye
Who spoke of the fire
Who entered the river
Who looked into the mirror
      and disappeared?

In whose room
does paper fall
wine turn sour?

"But you don't understand"
"different   concepts of   rhythm"
"The poem is Kansas"
"An elegy for a friend two years late"

Their names lie on the page like grave markers.
Let me speak them as if I knew the owners.

Aimee Anderson
Cindy Atwood
Willy Cromwell
Gary David
Bob Greene
J.L. McClure
Dana McMurry
Marne Rogers
Mark Thiessen
Linda Diane Warner

EGG POEM

We are eggs.

One of us holds
the magician's heart.

When the hero comes
he will crush us all.

PAPER POEM

Like a man in a foreign country
sentenced in a strange language,
forced to kneel and kiss the paper
whereon his punishment is written,

I kiss this paper.

SUNRISE

Here comes the sun
marching up over the hill
plain as you please
singing the same old song
as loud as he can.

He enters the house
freely as ever
kissing everybody
like an actress,
making the same
barbershop chatter.

"Yes sir,
yes sir.
You couldn't be more right
if you tried."

It's the same old toothpaste smile
and the same old slap on the back,

as if there were nobody missing,
as if he never left home.

PERSPECTIVE

I love people,
she said,
from a distance.

Everything in perspective.

Look over there toward the horizon.

No, no. More to your left.
Right where I'm pointing.

See it now,
that black dot in the landscape?

That's
my love.

THOSE I LOVE

Those I love —
even in my dreams
I see only their backs.

O, let me be there
with them
in a far country,

away from the hanging tongues
and the sheep faces
of those that love me.

CAUSE AND EFFECT

Because it is night

the moon impossible silver
the trees in shadow
praying to the true God
and you in my arms

because
it is night.

THE FIRST ANIMAL

The first animal
lives under my house.

When I sleep
it comes through the wall,
settles its bulk on my chest,
and puts its lips to mine.

It eats my breath.
When I die it will starve.

LUST

"Friend," it says, putting its fat hands
on my shoulders. "Friend . . . friend."

I move away.
"Keep your hands to yourself."

"But . . . but . . .
you taught me all I know."

BIRTHDAY POEM

1

I have eaten the year.
My tongue is black.

But doctors tell me there is no reason
why I cannot lead a normal existence

if I avoid strenuous exercise,
introspection, anger, and love.

So I ignore the year that lies
in my belly like an infected child.

2

All my candles burn.
I make my wish and blow.

One breath and they're out.

CLOCK

Who looks at a clock will find
the white reflection of his face.

His eyes have gone,
his nose and ears.

His hair has fallen,
his mouth become numerals

as he returns at 5:30
to stand before a mirror

which announces: behold
the egg has come home.

OPERA SEASON

You are invited to a masked ball.
Do not wear a mask.
No one will recognize you.

The king's mistress loses her slipper.
You stoop down to pick it up
and it is already gone.

Here comes the Barber of Seville.
he puts a towel around your neck
and slits your throat.

SORROW

1

Over my shoulder I see her
following from a distance

hair like a commercial
black boots and ridiculous cape.

Lose her in traffic
turn a corner

and there she is
straight ahead.

2

We pass in a crowd
strangers strangers.

She breathes in
about to speak.

No, I hiss,
Keep on walking.

I don't know you.
I don't know you.

3

But at night
when I'm alone

she comes
in faded pink pajamas

hair in curlers
with a bowl of popcorn.

The only woman
I'll ever love.

BITING MY FINGERNAILS

They are all coated with poison,
but when I am arrested I forget.

Please, I want to tell everything.
I am so anxious I bite my fingernails.

The chief of police comes in too late.
Too late he says in his heavy accent,
"We have a little surprise for you."

In comes my good gray-haired mother
who looks at me in disapproval and says,
"Don't bite your fingernails."

HONOR

Blood on my shoes
honor on my shoulders
like epaulets

I pass the children of smoke
who sit by the road
weaving a crown of thorns.

Is it for me, I cry, *for me?*

Yes, yes, they say.
Wear it with honor.

MORNING POEM

Every morning
light beats on my eyelids
like a hammer.

During the night
regret has died
in my mouth.
My breath smells
of its corpse.

If I have survived
I am not happy.

The knife
I have been sharpening
for my suicide
lies ready
on the kitchen table.

I use it
to cut my grapefruit.

RETURN

Three years buried
Love came back.

Where are my books?
Why did you burn my old clothes?
Didn't you know I would return?

SUMMER NIGHT

Along the road
the shadows of dogs
wait for the moon.

Mailboxes hold out
their empty hands.
Crickets sing
the hymn to silence.

The lonely, the abandoned
wrap themselves in ditches
and sleep.

Beyond the hill
the soft voice
of the mother of violence
is calling her children
home.

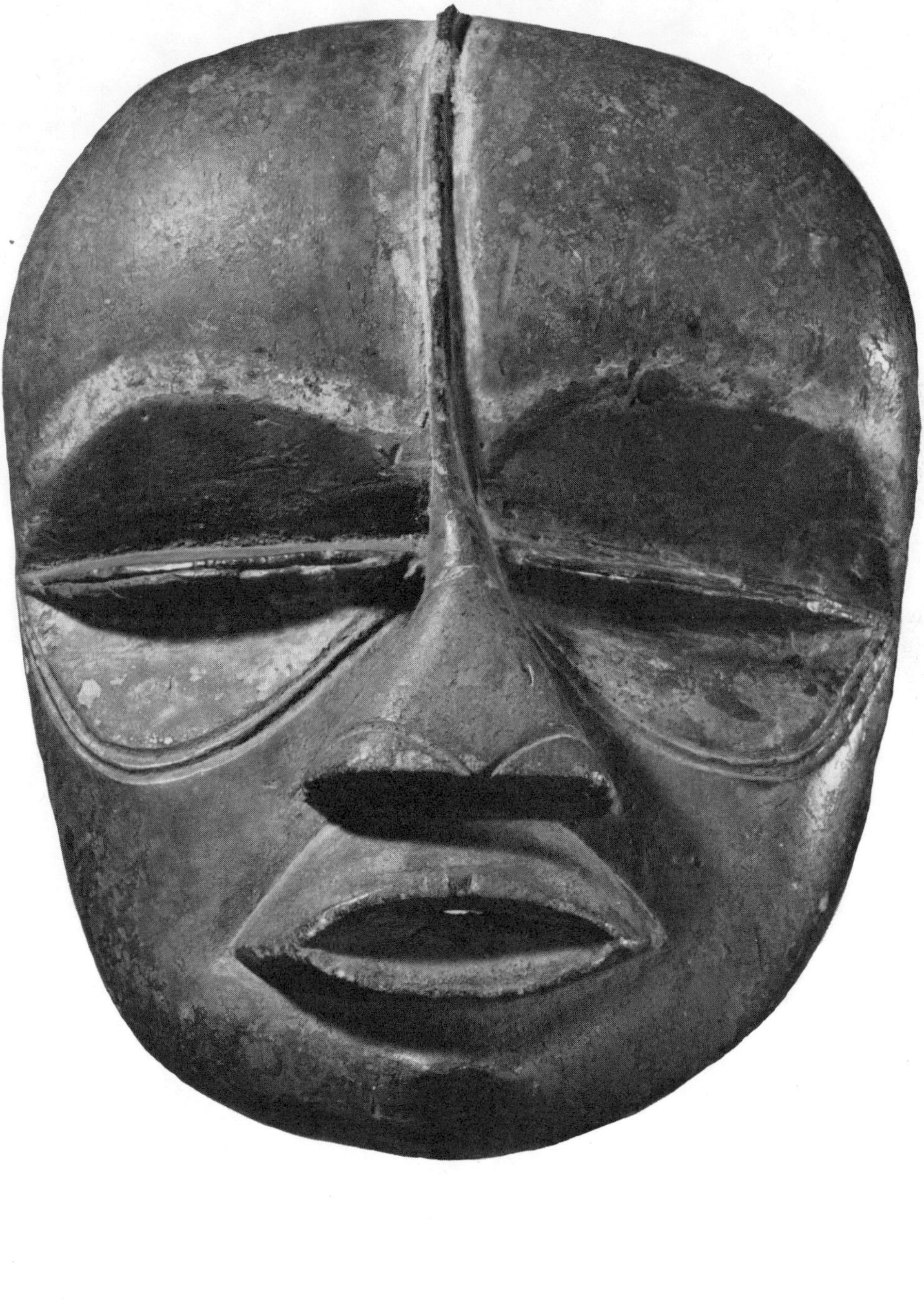